D1080228

Schools Library Service
Gwasaneth Llyfrgell
Ysgolion

HOLIDAYS AND FESTIVALS

Easter

Nancy Dickmann

www.raintreepublishers.co.uk
Visit our website to find out more information about Raintree books.

To order:
Phone 0845 6044371
Fax +44 (0) 1865 312263
Email myorders@raintreepublishers.co.uk

Customers from outside the UK please telephone +44 1865 312262

Raintree is an imprint of Capstone Global Library Limited, a company incorporated in England and Wales having its registered office at 7 Pilgrim Street, London, EC4V 6LB – Registered company number: 6695582

Text © Capstone Global Library Limited 2011
First published in hardback in 2011
The moral rights of the proprietor have been asserted.

All rights reserved. No part of this publication may be reproduced in any form or by any means (including photocopying or storing it in any medium by electronic means and whether or not transiently or incidentally to some other use of this publication) without the written permission of the copyright owner, except in accordance with the provisions of the Copyright, Designs and Patents Act 1988 or under the terms of a licence issued by the Copyright Licensing Agency, Saffron House, 6–10 Kirby Street, London EC1N 8TS (www.cla.co.uk). Applications for the copyright owner's written permission should be addressed to the publisher.

Edited by Sian Smith, Nancy Dickmann, and Rebecca Rissman
Designed by Steve Mead
Picture research by Elizabeth Alexander
Production by Victoria Fitzgerald
Originated by Capstone Global Library Ltd
Printed and bound in China by South China Printing Company Ltd

ISBN 978 0 431 00722 9
14 13 12 11 10
10 9 8 7 6 5 4 3 2 1

Tynnwyd o'r stoc
Withdrawn
AMAZON
DECEMBER
2010

British Library Cataloguing in Publication Data
Dickmann, Nancy.
Easter. -- (Holidays and festivals)
1. Easter--Pictorial works--Juvenile literature.
I. Title II. Series
394.2'667-dc22

Acknowledgements
We would like to thank the following for permission to reproduce photographs: Alamy pp. **10** (© Mikael Utterström), **13** (© Image Source), **20**, **23 middle** (© Anonymous Donor); Corbis pp. **4** (© Bob Sacha), **5**, **23 top** (© Jutta Klee), **7** (© Brooklyn Museum), **8** (© Fine Art Photographic Library), **9** (© Elio Ciol), **15** (© Fermin Cabanillas); Getty Images pp. **12** (Chris Graythen), **21** (Barbara Peacock/ Taxi); Photolibrary pp. **14** (ColorBlind/White), **16** (TAO Images Limited), **17** (Mark Edward Smith/Tips Italia), **18**, **23 bottom** (Paul Harris/John Warburton-Lee Photography), **19** (Juergen Richter/LOOK-foto); Shutterstock pp. **6**, **11** (© CURAphotography), **22 top left** (© 2happy), **22 top middle** (© Lobke Peers), **22 top right** (© Pierre Yu), **22 bottom left** (© Elena Schweitzer), **22 bottom right** (© Joshua Lewis).

Front cover photograph of Easter eggs reproduced with permission of Corbis (© Milk Photographie). Back cover photograph reproduced with permission of Alamy (© Anonymous Donor).

We would like to thank Diana Bentley, Dee Reid, Nancy Harris, and Richard Aubrey for their invaluable help in the preparation of this book.

Every effort has been made to contact copyright holders of material reproduced in this book. Any omissions will be rectified in subsequent printings if notice is given to the publishers.

Contents

What is a festival? 4
The story of Easter. 6
What happens at Easter? 12
Things to look for 22
Picture glossary 23
Index 24

What is a festival?

A festival is a time when people come together to celebrate.

Christian people celebrate Easter in the spring.

The story of Easter

Christian people believe Jesus is the son of God.

Jesus taught people to be kind and peaceful.

Some leaders did not like what he taught.

Jesus was killed.

Christian people believe Jesus then came back to life.

They believe this shows God's love for them.

What happens at Easter?

Before Easter, some people celebrate Mardi Gras.

They eat the foods that they plan to give up for Lent.

Lent lasts for 40 days. Lent is a time to think and pray.

On Good Friday, people remember the day Jesus died.

On Easter Sunday, people remember the day Jesus came back to life.

Some people sing happy songs in church.

Some people watch Easter parades.

Some people light special candles.

Some people decorate
Easter eggs.

Eggs are a sign of new life.

Things to look for

candle

chick

cross

eggs

rabbit

Have you seen these things? They make people think of Easter.

Picture glossary

Christian people people who follow the teachings of Jesus

decorate to make something look nice by putting colours or patterns on it

parade a line of people, walking along to celebrate or remember something

Index

Easter Sunday 16
eggs 20, 21, 22
God 6, 11
Good Friday 15
Jesus 6–10, 15, 16
Lent 13, 14

Notes for parents and teachers

Before reading

Ask the children if they know what holidays and festivals are. Brainstorm a list of festivals. Look at which festivals on the list are religious together. Christian people, who follow the religion of Christianity celebrate Easter. Some children from non-Christian or non-religious families may also celebrate Easter in a secular way.

After reading

• Show the children photos of Easter eggs from different cultures, such as Ukrainian pysanky, or even jewelled Fabergé eggs. Ask which symbols and decorations they might expect to find on Easter eggs. Help the children to design their own Easter eggs.

• Explain that Lent is the period of 40 days which comes before Easter. It is a season of reflection and preparation. Lent is often marked by fasting. Ask the children if there are things that they would find it hard to go without. Suggest they choose something (such as computer games or snacks) to give up for a day or a week. Afterwards, discuss what it was like to go without something they wanted.

• Discuss some of the pre-Lent celebrations around the world, such as Shrove Tuesday and Mardi Gras carnivals. Explain that these celebrations arose out of the need to use up foods that were not allowed during Lent. Help the children to make pancakes.